IRIDESCENT
WINGS

IRIDESCENT WINGS

RASO

MISTY RIDGE PRESS
MISSOULA, MONTANA

For information, contact

Misty Ridge Press
PO Box 8633
Missoula, MT 59807
www.mistyridgemedia.com

ISBN: 979-8-9851843-1-0
Cover and interior design by Open Heart Designs

To the great earth and her intricate web of beings,
who give and sustain life, and give us a place to love.

CONTENTS

This companion volume to the inward journey of *Winds of Silence* travels footpaths through the richness and complexity of living. How precious each moment, crystallized and irretrievable! My gratitude to friends, family, teachers and beloveds sharing this life's pathways.

"*The center clears. Knowing comes:*
The body is not singular like a corpse,
but singular like a salt grain
still in the side of the mountain."

—*Rumi*

INVIOLABLE GRACE

TOMATO POEM

the cherries are splitting their skins in the sun
beefsteaks are full and pack close to the stem
where the rich twangy smell of hot vines deepens
or lie swollen and languid on unskirted ground
grass and dark fainted leaves clinging moistly
to their undersides
as they bury themselves
sinking in abandoned silent union
toward winter soil

STORM ON THE WAY

high wind gusting through the grape arbor
tossing foxtails, rising through the broad leaves of small fruit trees
dandelion fairies careening through darkening afternoon skies
the wildness, the wind, the awaited

I putter through emptiness
emptiness, empty space, gathering clouds
flotsam of the neighborhood scudding down the street
sprinkler still walking across heat-baked grass
waiting until the emptiness overflows

it might, might not
grape vines tossing, tendrils whipping across the cyclone fence
mountain storm on the way, a flooding, wind-lashed storm
a drenching storm, if we're lucky,
or else such a passionate promise, with no embrace,
with no wetness, no culmination into dark, soaked earth,
no saturation, dry-breasted

A LIFTING OF DELICATE BRANCHES

full moon in a fluttery thin sky of clouds
my face on the window screen
a bit of cool air, and then

a lifting of delicate branches
lifting like dancers transported by grief
or darkness, or twilight, or mystery
I sit behind, feeling the movement within
the passion of movement, and darkness
hereness . . . here . . .
surrounding the passion like a cupping of petals
enclosing it in a vessel of no solidity

let the passion play with the instrument of my body
the uplifting of the delicate branch
moonlight, darkness, myself in a passion of watching
with a heart of clouded longing and mystery
it is bearable, it is music
surrounded by the fragrance of the rose

PROTECTION

this protection is so dour
couldn't I have chosen a more
flamboyant aspect to hide behind?

fleetness hides behind coolness
a dancer who
when not dancing
wears nun's shoes
the soles of my feet are tender
I have made myself a
thick skin suit
& don't stop for long unless I am alone

RULES

the nonpoetic
rules
but my soul craves
poetry

roool
rooooler
roooohhh
oooooh!!
the oooooooh
is what is missing

flat they made it flat
but life moves
moooooves
in poetry

in a poetic world
solutions cannot be found
in prose

INVIOLABLE GRACE

through, bindings, halting subjection
ended, this compromise
through and through

no baldheaded pilgrim I am
a madwoman with tangled hair
seeking union
passionate silence
movement consumed, burnt, revealed
inviolable grace

SPRING FEVER OBSERVED

Soft air, branches still bare,
bursts of pollen floating through sunlight.

Texaco self-serve, smell of gasoline
in the shadowed alcove
an Italian-looking man in running shorts
and polo shirt walks back to his car
glances at me, sunglasses pushed back on his head,
glances at me, in him too the hunger,
the roaring of the senses in civilized isolation.
I smile, avert my eyes.

The gut, the gut in turmoil.
The heart racing each time to the phone,
ringing all day, never for me,
never the lover who stirred the longing
that now moves in spring flood, in muddy flood,
through my limbs, through the organs within my flesh.

As if he came just to arouse the fibers of my skin.
As if he dropped by just to awaken the fever.
As if only the juices needed an object
to prove their functioning,
secrete themselves, endlessly secreting,
touching each part to a small flickering flame
of unruly power, loosening a heavy door
to the overripe cave of wanting, craving.

Craving.
Not painful in itself
but in abandoning the fall
to this sensation
that clings and burns.

Clings to something,
establishing craving.
Release just this!
Just this, the challenge.

THE OTHER

sticky skin, sticky heart
so she clears the space around her
let it be silent, let it be empty
clear the space so she can hear,
she can feel, she can see the pulse of life itself
without distortion, without the distortion of
her own center leaning, her own skin stretching
to accommodate, comfort, soothe or entertain
the Other

SNOW CRYSTALS

weak pale light
washes across the yard's white field
snow crystals turn inward
withdraw their points
dream of rivers
melt into a lacework
of tiny frozen streams

myself such a frozen archway
dreaming of soaked earth
yet held aloft by a season past

Concerns. Business.
The feeling of people and their needs.
Pressures of work to be done.
Relationships. Considerations.
Feeling back.
Hopeless. This time it's hopeless.
Feeling back.
Maybe it's time for a different approach.
Considerations and advice.
Feeling back.

Rain.
The swishing of car tires on wet pavement.

it doesn't rise today, but pools and opens
opens to moisture, fragrance
the back of the body, the pelvis and thighs
open to rain, wetness, earth, longing. . . .
longing
the body, the heart relinquish to wetness
and interpret it as pain
as needing some resolution
as needing the wet body of another

and if it is not pain?
if instead of cleaving to vibrating shape
it opens further?

"anytime you arrive is early"
charaiveti, charaiveti
go on, go on

AFTER THE HIGH SEAS

After the high seas almost drowned me
Had flung my heart against hard jagged rocks
While it quavered and cried for a different fate

Alone, cool moonlight spreads across a
Snowy land, spreading through my
Body too, pearlescent and resting,
Whole, grateful, alight.

BELLYACHING

When the center is missed
ALL is missed.
The rest is just bellyaching
and the trickling of tears.

THIS PRECIOUS LIFE

GREETING

The day moves by among shining leaf shadows
through bright green trembling
one dark side to another

images melt in the sharp heat
slip into a violet pool
trickle toward me in an indigo finger
drop by drop from a dry twig

words like budding clouds blow
sweep up the steep cliffs of my arms
they do not billow into form but
float wisp-like about my shoulders

today I crackle with dust and sage
in an afternoon filled with wonderings
I mold a greeting from dry creek pebbles
which, wrapped in a new green leaf,
I toss to a streaming sunbeam
to fly to you
with my love

EASTER IN HAYWARD

gold stripes
pin stripes
gilt stripes falling
through a skirt with inlaid pleats
and delicate piping
starched pretty daughter
smiling in the side yard for photos
preferring to be wilder

pancake breakfast in a lodge on a hill
in gold Hayward hills under cerulean sky
the rough wood floor sounds hollow when you walk
and there's a steamy feeling along the serving line
not much of interest except the atmosphere
the atmosphere, the feeling in the air,
camaraderie in the air, the feeling on my skin,
sunny day, bright air, golden hills,
and inside
the men flipping flapjacks

THE LAST NIGHT AT NEW BRIGHTON BEACH
after three months camping above the Pacific
with Thunder the cat

on the last night
a full moon
shadows overlaid like pine needles
yesterday only it was new again

every sunset hour following a clear day
the ocean becomes that exquisite
shimmering blue
waves suck in dark breaths
and exhale in foam
Thunder and I sit on our beacon stump perch
dangling our feet over the infinite

yesterday it was the new moon
the new moon sailing

forest home
newly greened
the sun has slipped
the iceplant begins to bloom
the tide sweeps over the beach
the rains have started

I will miss
the wind
in your streaming branches

LULLABY

golden splashing
silken wind

I gather the vastness
        gently coaxing
I put it all in one small berry
My gift to you

                golden splashing
                silken wind

Feel the universe sleepily unfold inside you
        filling you with clear, infinite space
See how large and beautiful you've grown
Soon you will be everywhere
        luminous with starlight

                golden splashing
                silken wind

THE MILKY WAY

highway sounds
breaker sounds
when the lantern goes out
a bright banner across the sky
    The Milky Way!

        Father's voice is hushed
        we crunch along the path
        breathing deeply
        cold cheeks
        turning from fiery fairy cities
        to thrilling night
            The Milky Way!

a blessing for us this starry night
beyond the final shadow flickerings
night is a pageant just begun
I fling away my sober selves
    The Milky Way!

        to which corner
        of the star-draped ballroom
        will I be whisked tonight?

ON MISMALOYA BEACH WITH MY MOTHER

from the length of my life I recognize
your strong even crawl
in this tropical ocean, too,
Mismaloya

soft water, soft air, soft pools of color
pale sky streaked with clouds
on shore the palapas
a sky-skier about to embark to fly
along red-roofed cliffs forested with palms
all this, even just met, can be familiar
but your face
as you stop swimming and turn toward me
without history, uncomposed
is new, fresh, vital

for this moment there is no detour
no interruption
no abduction of clarity by words or feelings
no maze, no celebration, no recrimination
no shadow, but only the depth of carving
but simply the flood of light of being
illuminating the lines and planes of your beauty

within yourself containing yourself
"small as a mustard seed, great as the tree of heaven"
as you contained me, subsequent paradox of time
we are fitfully dreaming
we are struggling toward birth
through inner eyes I see our unending blossoming

FULL MOON HEAT

full moon heat
mid-May high noon
hawks over browning hills
ruby-throats under eaves

my warbling life
I exhale thee
song of wandering melodies
arc of prismed light
heat wraps me in thin sweat and rustles on
new pears are budding in their smooth green skins

the moon peaks in her orbit
unseen in California
crowning over the East China Sea
in a few hours her ancient watery pathway
will stretch here over our ocean
here, where now long swells glint paley
the shining one will move toward and beyond us
lessened by a hairsbreadth
trailing stars and tides

full moon heat
mid-May high noon
ruby-throats singing under eaves

ISOSCELES PEAK

Clambering over granite
glancing up into blue
The new moon rising
from the top of Isosceles Peak
as a pale crown

GARGOYLES

Caution and Wariness
the gargoyles of my heart
watch you
they are silent
they examine your intent
they appraise us both
nothing slips by

too early for love
too soon for trust
each in each
is isolated

oh I write you a love letter
too soft for the stern to feel or grasp
carelessly I spill joy like petals
carried on a whisper to the
bright spot between us

I am a fool
I scramble foolishly behind
we are not ready yet
for this naked light

EXPOSURE

fear comes with exposure
with any position stated

because its elements of truth
are contradicted as spoken
with its elements of untruth

exposed with a statement
which constricts reality
to a stick figure
and in a ludicrous posture

I didn't mean it like that exactly
and also I did
close the
exposure

SANGHA

feelings upwelling
I am closed in, collapsed
tiny, sad
tears flowing and flowing
layerings of reserve kept me apart
now weeping remnants of
loneliness and loss

grief pushes upward,
meets the heart, swelling it
so a flat landscape
becomes hilly
rounded, smooth, furry with grasses
a landscape of green and mist
eyes the rivulets, overflowing

my friend sits near me
holds my hand
strokes my hair
almost we are sitting on the misty path
when I look in her eyes
she is crying too
smiles & tears & mystery

MANGO RAINS

waking in darkness, fan whirring
a feeling of movement
sound just beyond recognition

wetness
trees tossing
rain

MANGO RAINS II

velvet breeze, humid, even coolish
sleeping without a fan, and with a sheet
sky just twilit now
birds singing and singing
in the street a rickshaw bounces along

BUTTERFLIES

words flutter in my mouth
like butterflies, gentle, sweet
from every limb, from my heart, skin
from the soles of my feet, the backs
of my legs, from inside
from outside like a thirst
carrying its own quenching
breath moves through my body
an interior wind of loving

something intercedes, resisting birth
that which is unspoken fills my mouth
with an iridescence that longs and
fears to reach toward itself

is it itself it reaches toward
or am I lost again in dream

will I forget the vast lonely wildness
languages of water and stone

will you turn away from my tenderness
shimmering dust on wings of solitude

will I lose my way to
the depth, the silence
dark source of all I know of love

FEET

My feet look like my mother's now
The crooked big toe with its knob of bunion
on a basically similar structure
The bones of our faces—
When I catch a glimpse in a mirror
I see her reflected there.
Ending with me, those long-toed, high-arched feet,
those bones of the facial structure.

And what is my responsibility?
To hold you? or to let you go?
Or somehow, in this inutterable complexity
to hold you *and*
to let you go
remember you *and*
allow the dream
the soap bubble
to dissolve
as if it had never been
as if this *I* had never been
this story
remembered and dissolved
simultaneously.

CONCENTRIC SHALLOW ARCHES

concentric shallow arches
of blackened drizzled branches
slender in lucent twilight
rimed in thaw-heavy snow
catching this

lichen in ruffled circlets
dark drooped limb
evening on a dimming path

a small shluff
white through white
dropping unseen
high frond gently waving

a tremor through my legs
stirs a tiny blaze
womb streaked orange
shadows weaving and whispering
alive

a slender lily blooms in the breast
arms are rivers
and all without effort
alive

YOUR EYES

Your eyes
give me another dimension of living
what you see
how you see
catching the particularity
of light, form, composition
attuned to beauty
alert to some newly available angle or
vista or a wild being in mosaic of place

Your eyes
bestow a richness of view
that opens the dimensions of my world
and I have come to trust and rely upon them
an expanded home with its own unique access
to the marvelous, the delicate, the evanescent

My eyes have their own native way
and that intrinsically is enough
as all is contained in each particularity
so nothing finally is lost
the whole available now
as soughing wind stirs the branches of the pines
and sunlight gleams along long needles
warms mottled bark
soaks into the shadow-streaked ground
where last year's grasses tremble

It is enough, it surely would be enough
to see through these eyes
let them empty into the whole

unobstructed
uninterrupted
by human sharing
by intraspecies delight

From an unseen tree spire
startling melodious song
wren lands on the small solar panel
nonfunctional for a decade
that juts from the old shed roof
wren bobs there, chittering a little,
peering into the roof peak cavity

Enough, yet the heart of paradise opens
in multidimensionality of view
sharing, even through silent touch,
the soul's movement into awe

ON THE LAND

HAWTHORN

Hawthorn blooms in tiny cream circlets,
neat, not touseled as the
service berry who now scatters petals
over soaked green ground.
A fine rain drums lightly on the tent.
Flycatcher sings dryly from an unseen branch.

MEASUREMENT

Falling into *this*
MacGillivray's warbler sings unseen
from the forest's edge
New foliage on service berry
opens pale lips to drink air
with pores just born
The back opens, falls away
toward a timeless abyss

Can I measure it?
Dole out a portion
and re-coagulate to a
productive human being?
Can it be a utility, a part
of the life
or must it
swallow me whole?

circled together loosely
as each feels to be
the skin of the land
opens

our hands have felt
its scratchy surface
carried its wood, breathed
its scent, piled its green
branches high for burning
hauling, gathering
treading paths
in conversation
and alone

now circled together loosely
in every kind of chair
on barely greening springtime ground
cooler of beer, wine bottles opened
black bean enchiladas and
raspberry rhubarb pie

the heart of the land
opens
we are held
circled together
loosely

THE MOON NOW UNDER HALF

The moon now under half
floated far below the horizon
when I headed out with pillow and blanket
for the season's sleeping space, a tent.
Sky was black, and glittering with stars,
and the ribbon of the Milky Way
meandered across the expanse.
Summer sky is rarely so dark,
the trailings of our galaxy most often unseen
through the unfathomable distance.

Hours later I awoke, in a luxury of comfort,
large screen windows sieving a cool breeze
that rustled the tent fly as it slipped across the ground.
Low on the horizon, through pine and fir,
a clear silver light pierced the starless forest.

I pulled my body from its soft cocoon
and clambored out the U-shaped door.
Swirls of illumined cloud spangled the sky,
lit by a moon now gleaming, now hidden,
impossibly low yet casting pale brilliance
in long low streaks, splashing over trees,
the sky in a vast turning dance.

When will I trust the unfurling of change,
glittering night sky becoming cloud-swept with moonlight,
yielding to a morning of this later season
where robin alone still sings?

In noon heat dragonfly visits
and reveals her translucent,
iridescent wings.

THE BLESSED RISK

So delicate,
as the attention settles.
It flurries, like small birds startling off a still lake,
and then again, returning.
Scent of water, dank smell of wet,
and the traveling fragrance of soil and forest,
concentric ripples spreading out
across glassy green and gold

The risk — to remain.

Patience to remain
while primed to respond
to myriad hooks, myriad calls.
A warbler singing from the serviceberry.
Attention darts, does not wait,
is not still. Darts back. Hooks to lists,
conversations, demands, hopes.
Darts, does not settle, flickers off again.

Patience not as a moral dictum
but a state of being at rest.
Remaining.
The blessed risk.

LILAC LEAF

deck frosted from the night's hard freeze
pines still against undifferentiated gray
a raven pumps its wings through the air like bellows

bare sketch of a rustle
lilac leaf releases
taps and tumbles to the ground

REQUIEM FOR TREES
In the aftermath of wind

it snows
the land closes in on itself
closing within a blanket of white
its scars hidden, held inward
cooled and covered
inward turning

let us be now
let us be for now
we will heal
we will burgeon forth with spring
but not today
not this day

where tractor tires have ground us
into tread-furrowed mud and
deep crosshatches of chain
we will pause a little longer
our sighs compressed
our shiny borders of kinnick kinnick and
sleeping violets will drift as memory
in this season's turning

our landscape is stilled
the bodies of our majestic ones
the fragrant elders
the root of our song
have been dragged across the broken ground
their branches in heaps

their torn roots still splayed lifeless in air
skidded across the broken service berry
the crushed reachings of snowberry
to orderly piles in machine-made mud

but it snows
white covers the land

we close
let us be for now
in our newly naked state
raw and wounded
our fragrant waving heartland reduced
to a few spindly survivors
with most of their limbs
sheared off
when the majestic ones fell
crashing to the earth
in a keening ferocity
a narrow keening ferocity
of wind

let us remember for a time
let us close in the dying
of what we were
breathe a while in the dark and silence
hidden beneath gently falling snow
hidden in the turning
toward new life

LIFE OF LIGHT

sun emerges in a halo of cloud
beyond forest and before forest
winterlight low across and through
a landscape drenched and drifted in
snow, then crusted by January rain,
the gathered cold that held the
morning close now permeated by
low long rays of warmth

the plane of my cheek swells
to meet the life of light

if that was, then perhaps
the note of living and her corollaries
will be heard
imbibed
returned

DIPPER DANCE

Fog has risen above the treetops
leaving pines flocked in crystalline sleeves.
Woodpecker taps along the bare streak
on an ancient one where lightning seared
a naked gash, crumbled at the bottom as if
chewed by beetles, crown still green
within its sheathing of ice.

Yesterday the fog hovered aloft until
midafternoon, when I set off on a walk,
tying on boots, hefting my pack, slipping
gloved hands through the straps of trekking poles.
I hiked upward as the fog descended,
the long tail of my braid a tassel of frost.

Swinging along the upper ditch road
scallops of ice edged the flowing water,
now running low in its rough canal,
with concentric ovals and frozen ripples
snow-flowers scattered in circular clumps.
I walked steadily, poles clicking
on brittle ground.

An abrupt movement on the bank.
Whirring of wings.

Dipper has appeared on the edge of the ice,
sleek and dark, regarding the walker,
who has stilled, regarding the dipper.
The assessment is neutral.

Her gaze returns to the stream, beak down.
She bobs, dips, dunks her head quickly
in and out of the rippling current,
dives, disappears, reemerges
to whir to a shelf of frozen lace
backed by the bank's long low arch.

Then she began her dance.

She ran along the fragile edge
as fingers tap across a table
drumming with tiny agile feet
a pattern of hollow resonant steps
that boomed quietly through the
stream's amphitheatre.
Up and down the scalloped shelf she
shaped and molded her creation—

Run, pause, stamp a little....
Bob, dunk, stamp.... run....
Skid on a slick patch....
Walk an invisible frozen bridge,
Whir to the bank, pause....
and dance again—
Stamping an intricate improvised rhythm
into the fog that flocked my hair
and returned her inspired drumming
to her ears and to mine.

Grateful kudos for your masterpiece!
Human hands get cold in thin gloves.
I bow and descend toward warmth.

CLEAR LIGHT

an inch of new snow
23 degrees
sun a golden ball
gleaming through the trees
clear light

foliage glistening
dark trunks rising
rising through layers
of glistening white

It's not me!
not me!
I cannot perceive it!

"don't lean out"
"keep the weight back"

Isness
It is
Glory hallelujah

WAXING MOON

moon waxing to nearly full
in a clear sky
but still it snags in the tops
of the pines
casts shadows across the land
shadows cast across
a silvery land

THE PRICE

First day of summer, fragrant and fresh
after yesterday's rain. I sit in the cool shade
of the two pines, near fading lilacs that
waft their heavenly perfume through illuminated grasses
around and by me across the wet ground.

A junco landed on my bare foot!
Suddenly, from behind, it touched down lightly,
flashed off into the lilacs, disappeared into low greenery.

In silence is the answer.
Millions of times remembered, millions of times forgotten.
Remembered, but no longer felt, the words themselves
disconnected, disembodied, regarded with curiosity
or desperation, with unseeing eyes.
And remembered again.

The price. There is a price.
Everything. All.
The very self, the very perspective,
that strains and covets and hopes and works responsibly.
Allowing the vertigo, familiar and strange...
forbidden.

ACKNOWLEDGMENTS

A deep thank you to Jamie Tipton of Open Heart Designs for her wonderful work on this and so many other projects of the heart. Thank you to friends, family and beloveds who have walked these meandering pathways with me, sharing your insight, delight, tears and laughter. To the mystic Osho, gratitude is unending.

Raso grew up on the western edge of the North American continent where ocean tides, ancient forest and high alpine wilderness became her lifetime teachers. From an early age she was drawn to an ecstatic and expressive path, which was tempered and enhanced by the disciplines of Aikido and a committed path of meditation. Her other works include *Winds of Silence*, a companion volume of poetry; *Alaya, Songs for Earth and Sky*, an offering of music; and *Voice*, a multimedia play exploring effects of the McCarthy era in the United States from a child's perspective. Raso lives in western Montana, where she tends with her partner an area of forested land, teaches Aikido, plays music and continues walking the pathless path of meditation and love.